Kindness

Ashley Lee

Explore other books at:
WWW.ENGAGEBOOKS.COM

VANCOUVER, B.C.

e →WWW.ENGAGEBOOKS.COM

Kindness: Good Character Traits
Lee, Ashley, 1995 –
Text © 2024 Engage Books
Design © 2024 Engage Books

Edited by: A.R. Roumanis
Design by: Mandy Christiansen

Text set in Myriad Pro Regular.
Chapter headings set in Anton.

FIRST EDITION / FIRST PRINTING

LIBRARY AND ARCHIVES CANADA CATALOGUING IN PUBLICATION

Title: Kindness / Ashley Lee.
Names: Lee, Ashley, author.
Description: Series statement: Good Character Traits

Identifiers: Canadiana (print) 20230446973 | Canadiana (ebook) 20230446981
ISBN 978-1-77878-663-1 (hardcover)
ISBN 978-1-77878-664-8 (softcover)
ISBN 978-1-77878-665-5 (epub)
ISBN 978-1-77878-666-2 (pdf)

This project has been made possible in part by the Government of Canada.

Canada

Kindness

Contents

What Is Kindness?

Kindness means doing nice things for other people.

It also means saying nice things instead of mean things.

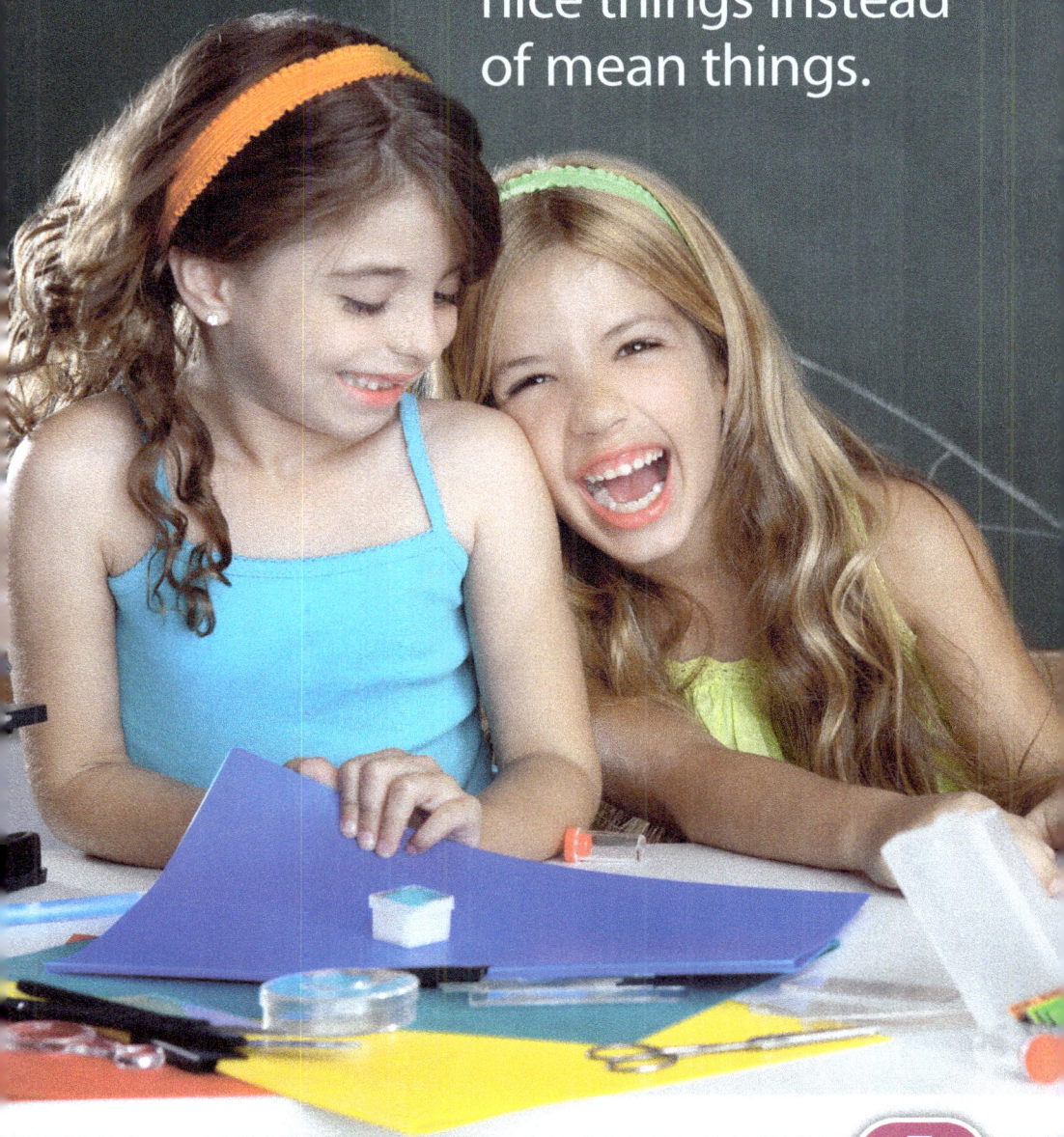

Why Is Kindness Important?

Being kind makes other people happy.

People share
their happiness
by being kind
to others.

What Does Kindness Look Like?

Kind people help others.

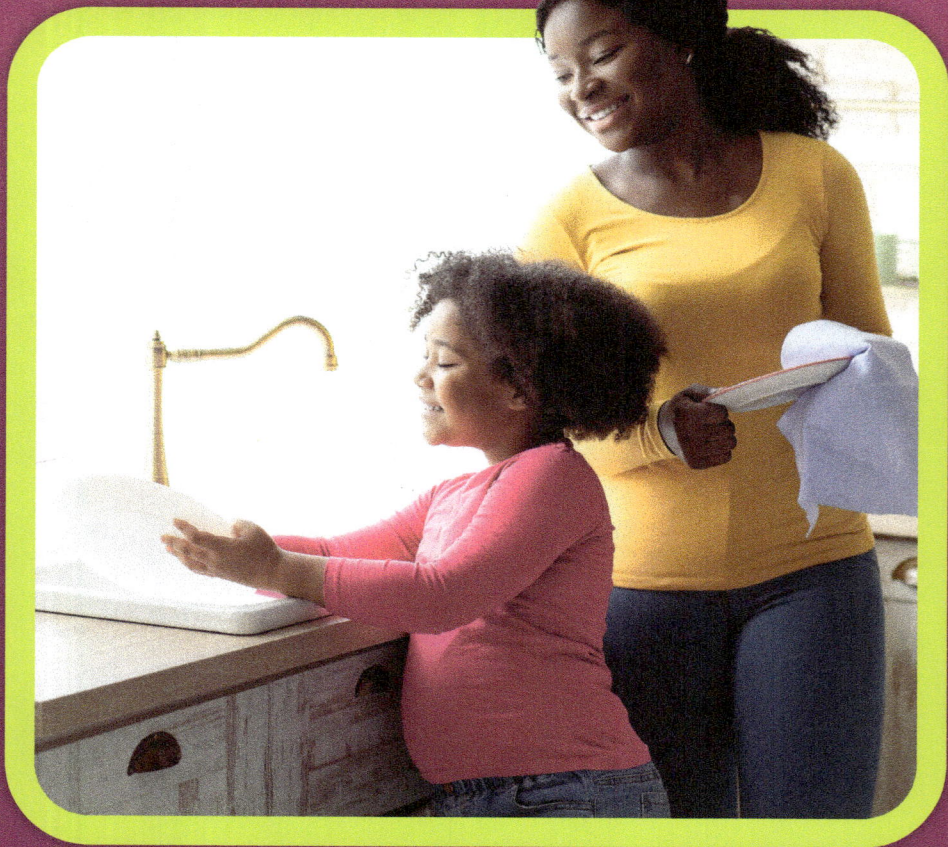

They are not mean to other people.

How Does Kindness Affect You?

Being kind can make you feel happy.

It feels good to help other people.

How Does Kindness Affect Others?

Being kind makes other people want to be kind too.

It lets people know you **care** about them.

Key Word

Care: like someone and want them to be happy.

Is Everyone Kind?

Sometimes people forget to be kind.

Be kind to them. This can help them remember to be kind to others.

Is It Bad if You Are Not Kind?

It is okay if you forget to be kind sometimes.

Remember to say sorry and try to be kind next time.

Does Kindness Change Over Time?

The act of being kind does not change over time.

But some people become more or less kind as they get older.

Is It Hard to Be Kind?

It can be hard to be kind if you do not like someone.

Being kind will get easier if you **practice**.

Key Word

Practice: do something over and over again so you get better at it.

How Can You Learn to Be Kinder?

Think about what you are going to say or do before you do it.

Ask yourself if what you are going to say or do is kind.

Be kind!

Be Nice!

How Can You Help Others Be Kinder?

Help others by showing them what kindness looks like.

Share your toys, say kind words, and be a good friend.

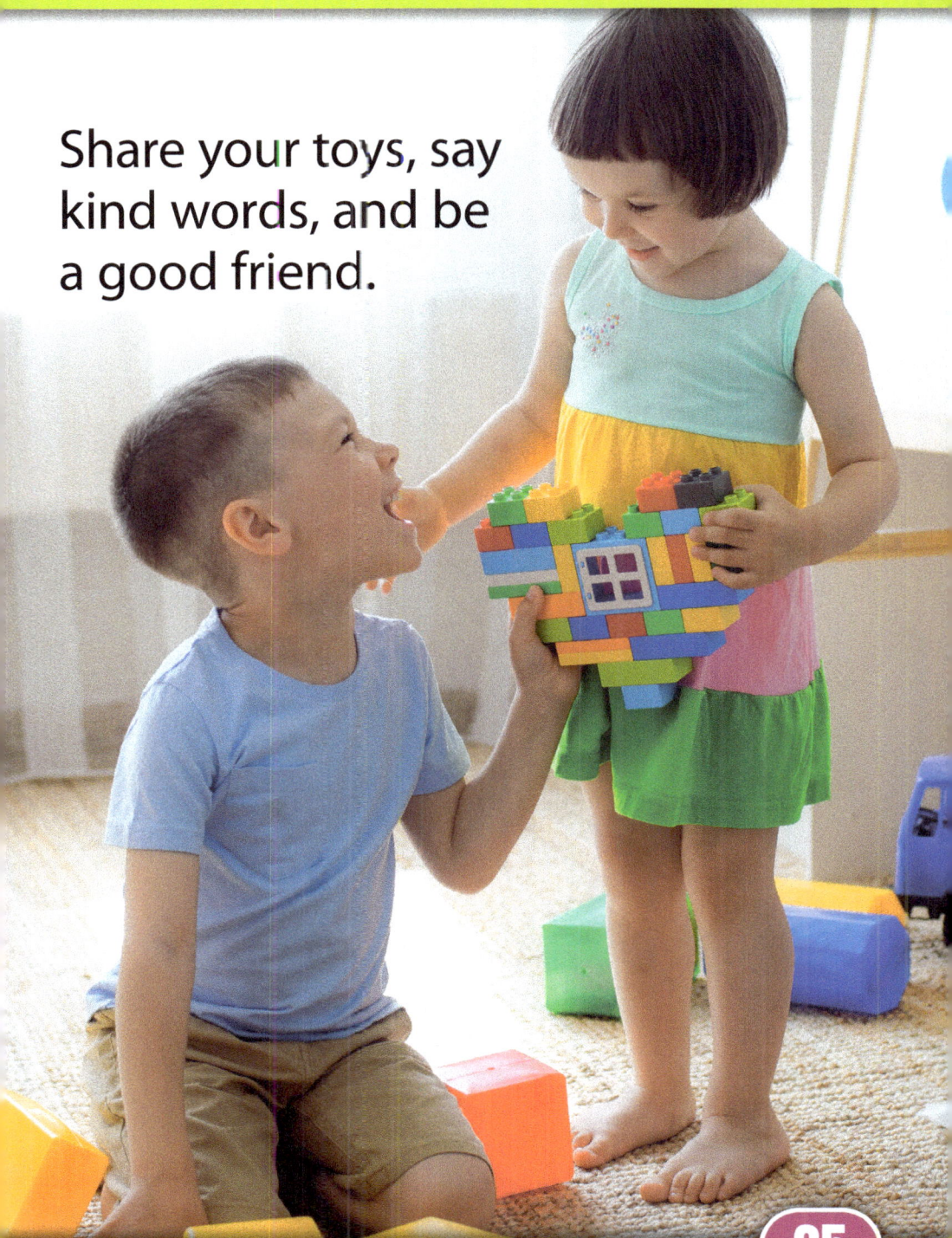

How to Be Kind Every Day

1. Clean up garbage.

2. Hold the door open for someone else.

3. Let someone know they did a good job.

4. Tell someone you like being around them.

Kindness Around the World

Big storms sometimes **damage** people's homes.

Kind people from around the world will help **rebuild** these homes.

Key Word

Rebuild: build something again.

Quiz

Test your knowledge of kindness by answering the following questions. The questions are based on what you have read in this book. The answers are listed on the bottom of the next page.

1 Does being kind make other people happy?

2 Are kind people mean to other people?

3 Does it feel good to help other people?

4 Can being kind make other people want to be kind?

5 Is it okay if you forget to be kind sometimes?

6 Will being kind get easier if you practice?

Explore Other Pre-1 Readers.

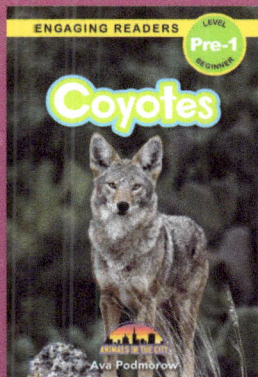

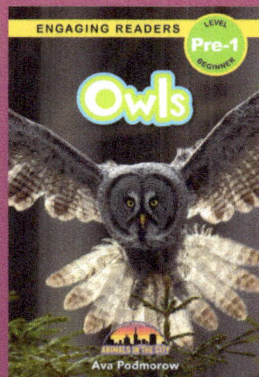

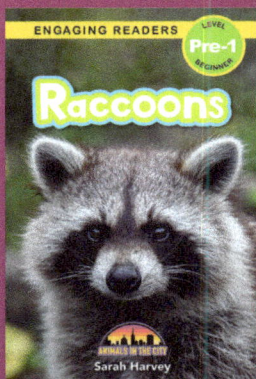

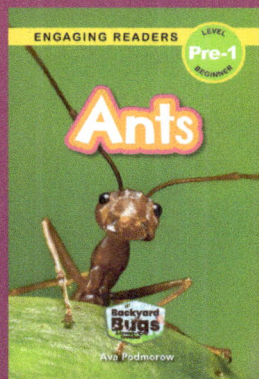

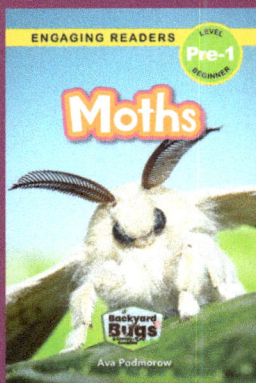

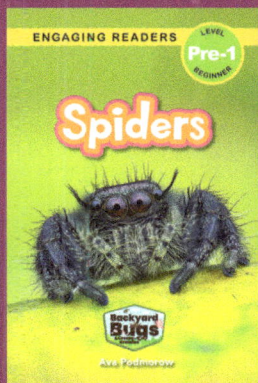

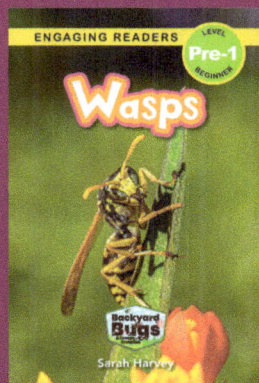

ENGAGING READERS — LEVEL Pre-1 BEGINNER
Cats
ANIMALS IN THE CITY
Ava Podmorow

ENGAGING READERS — LEVEL Pre-1 BEGINNER
Coyotes
ANIMALS IN THE CITY
Ava Podmorow

ENGAGING READERS — LEVEL Pre-1 BEGINNER
Owls
ANIMALS IN THE CITY
Ava Podmorow

ENGAGING READERS — LEVEL Pre-1 BEGINNER
Raccoons
ANIMALS IN THE CITY
Sarah Harvey

ENGAGING READERS — LEVEL Pre-1 BEGINNER
Skunks
ANIMALS IN THE CITY
Ava Podmorow

ENGAGING READERS — LEVEL Pre-1 BEGINNER
Ants
Backyard Bugs
Ava Podmorow

ENGAGING READERS — LEVEL Pre-1 BEGINNER
Moths
Backyard Bugs
Ava Podmorow

ENGAGING READERS — LEVEL Pre-1 BEGINNER
Spiders
Backyard Bugs
Ava Podmorow

ENGAGING READERS — LEVEL Pre-1 BEGINNER
Wasps
Backyard Bugs
Sarah Harvey

Visit www.engagebooks.com/readers

www.ingramcontent.com/pod-product-compliance
Lightning Source LLC
Chambersburg PA
CBHW051237020426
42331CB00016B/3416